CHARLOTTE

Basketball
Great Moments, Records, and Facts
by Teddy Borth

ABDO
GREAT SPORTS
Kids

abdopublishing.com

Published by Abdo Kids, a division of ABDO, PO Box 398166, Minneapolis, Minnesota 55439.

Printed in the United States of America, North Mankato, Minnesota.

102014

012015

THIS BOOK CONTAINS
RECYCLED MATERIALS

Photo Credits: AP Images, Getty Images, Shutterstock,
© Mayskyphoto / Shutterstock p.5, © User:Zibby42 / CC-SA-3.0 p.7

Production Contributors: Teddy Borth, Jennie Forsberg, Grace Hansen

Design Contributors: Laura Rask, Dorothy Toth

Library of Congress Control Number: 2014943709

Cataloging-in-Publication Data

Borth, Teddy.

 Basketball : great moments, records, and facts / Teddy Borth.

   p. cm. -- (Great sports)

ISBN 978-1-62970-688-7 (lib. bdg.)

Includes bibliographical references and index.

1. Basketball--Juvenile literature.   I. Title.

796.323--dc23

               2014943709

Table of Contents

Basketball

A gym teacher came up with basketball in 1891. It was raining. He wanted to keep his students busy.

5

Basketball Courts

Basketball is played all over

the world. Courts can be

inside or outside.

7

Great Records

Kareem Abdul-Jabbar has the high score for basketball. He has 38,387 points over 20 years. Karl Malone is second. He has 36,928 points.

9

Bill Russell has the most **title** wins. He played for 13 seasons. He won 11 titles. All were with the Boston Celtics.

The 1995–96 Chicago Bulls

had the best season.

They won 72 games.

They lost only 10 games.

Wilt's 100-Point Game

Wilt Chamberlain holds many **records**. On March 2, 1962, he had one of his best nights.

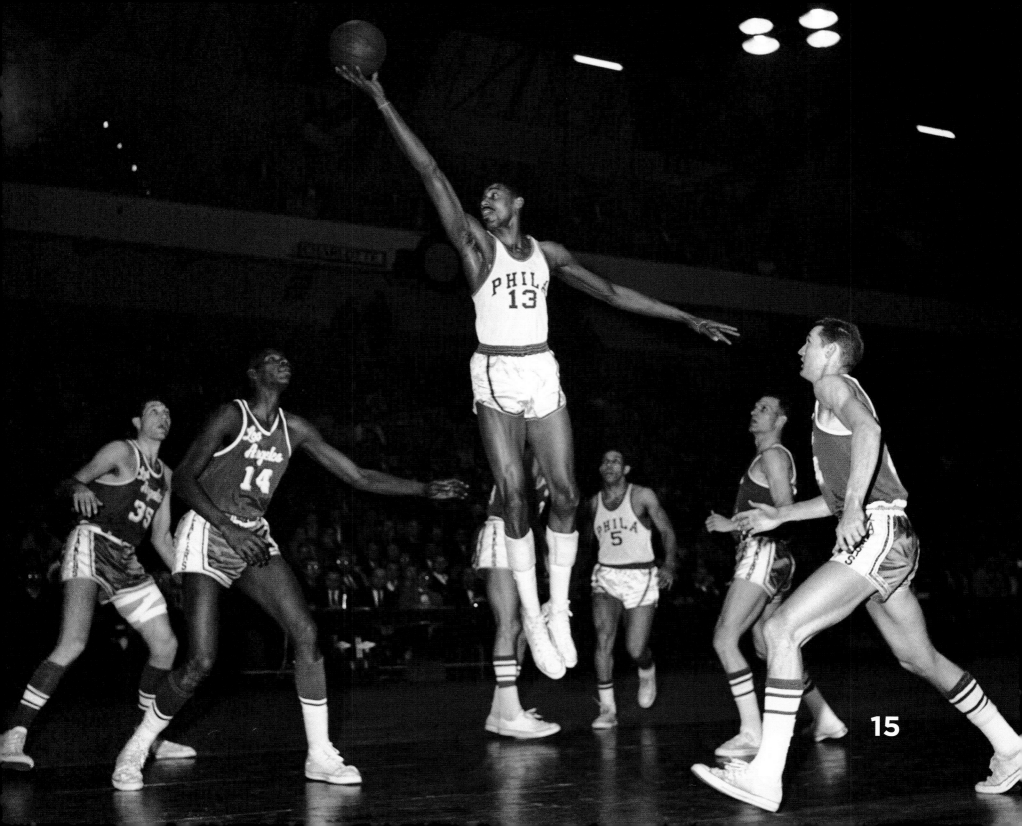

15

Wilt scored 100 points in one game. Nobody has come close since.

1998 NBA Finals

On June 14, 1998, the Bulls
are playing for the title. They
are losing to the Jazz by one
point. There are 19 seconds left.
Michael Jordan makes his move.

19

Jordan **steals** the ball from

Karl Malone. Jordan shoots

with 5 seconds left. He scores!

The Jazz take one last shot.

The ball does not go in.

The Bulls win the trophy!

21

More Facts

- Wilt Chamberlain has an average of 50.4 points per game. This is the highest of any player.

- Michael Jordan played a 1997 championship game with the flu. He made the final shot that won the game!

- The 1992 USA Olympic basketball team is called the "Dream Team." They beat everybody by an average of 44 points that year. Team USA has earned 21 gold medals in basketball (men and women). That is 17 more than the next ranked country.

Glossary

championship – a contest to find the best team.

record – the best accomplishment in a sport.

steal – to take the ball away from another player.

title – given to the first-place team.

Index

abdokids.com

Use this code to log on to abdokids.com and access crafts, games, videos and more!

Abdo Kids Code:
GBK6887